BOOK
ARCADE

FIRST
BOOK
ARCADE
OPENED
IN THE
WORLD

A MILLION
BOOKS

COLE'S BOOK ARCADE

COLE'S
BOOK
ARCADE

Our Country Cousin.

E.W.COLE

Chasing the Rainbow

Lisa Lang

ARCADE
PUBLICATIONS

Published by Arcade Publications
166A Amess St
Carlton North VIC 3054 Australia
www.arcadepublications.com

Designed by Michael Brady
Printed by Griffin Press
Distributed by Dennis Jones & Associates

National Library of Australia Cataloguing-in-Publication entry

Lang, Lisa.
E.W. Cole: Chasing the rainbow.

ISBN 9780980436709 (pbk.).

1. Cole, E. W. (Edward William), 1832-1918. 2. Booksellers
and bookselling - Victoria - Melbourne - Biography. 3. Publishers
and publishing - Victoria - Melbourne - Biography. I. Title.

381.45002092

With assistance from

Supported by

Contents

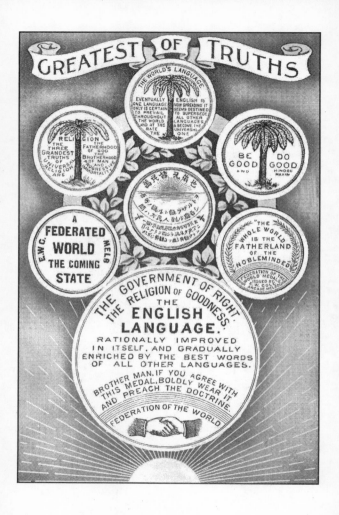

INTRODUCTION

Edward Cole caused some controversy when he trade-marked the rainbow in 1874. Some people believed that the rainbow was a Christian symbol – the sign of God's covenant – and should not be used to make money. Preachers berated him from their pulpits, and Edward received some angry letters. He held his ground. He plastered the rainbow's image across the white façade of his Bourke Street Book Arcade, and across the cover of *Cole's Funny Picture Book*. His plain-dressing wife wore a rainbow brooch at her throat.

The history books are filled with men searching for their pot of gold. Men seeking land, trade routes, precious materials, vast riches. Some men found their pots of gold in Victoria during the 1850s gold rush – the decade when hundreds of thousands of excited gold seekers came to Victoria. Among the hopeful was Edward William Cole. Edward never found much gold, but he turned out to be a brilliant entrepreneur.

Publicity was his specialty. In the 1870s most businesses treated newspaper advertising as little more than an extension of pinning a notice to a tree. Ads were straightforward and factual. But Edward's ads were playful, silly and actively engaged the reader – so much so that they once caused an edition of the *Herald* newspaper to sell out. He grasped the potential of advertising like a man who had grown up with Coca Cola and television, not one born into 1830s rural England and taught to read with the family Bible.

For all his business acumen, Edward was also an idealist. In his Book Arcade, customers were encouraged to read for as long as they liked. Books were damaged and stolen, and a magistrate once criticised his policy for its attractiveness to thieves. But if the easy atmosphere encouraged thieves, it also encouraged the poor and uneducated to read without intimidation. This mattered to Edward. He believed in world peace, equality and education for all, and he believed these were all achievable within a few generations. No wonder he loved the rainbow: symbol of peace, harmony and diversity.

But the rainbow is also an ideal: perfect, unattainable, forever out of reach.

This is Edward's story. The story of a man who went looking for a pot of gold, and ended up chasing the rainbow.

1 COLE'S CORDIALS

When Edward Cole arrived in Melbourne, the Yarra River was crowded with ships, and their swaying masts and riggings formed a vast, skeletal forest against the sky. He stepped from a small schooner, packed with 50 gold seekers, and onto the wharf at Spencer Street. After six weeks at sea, Edward had grown thin from living off tinned meat and salt junk, and his legs were as jellied and as useless as the legs in a dream. But he was lucky. Another ship, the *Ticonderoga*, which had arrived a week earlier, was so rotten with typhus and dysentery that 168 passengers had died. The only fever Edward carried off the boat was gold fever.

Gold fever was highly contagious. It spread by word of mouth and newspapers. Edward caught it in South Africa. If he'd read of the massive gold deposits in Victoria, then he'd probably also read how easy it was to dig it up. Honest labour in a charming, pastoral setting. Easy as hoeing a field. Ninety-four thousand people raced to Victoria in 1852, on anything that sailed, and Edward was one of them. He landed in Melbourne on 12 November 1852.

Edward was 20 and wanted to make his fortune. He'd failed to make it hawking sandwiches on the streets of London, or working as a farmhand in South Africa. All he had was a pouch full of savings and a single friend, Henry Smith, whom he'd met on the boat. They departed the bustling wharf together, and left behind the other new arrivals who were spreading out their belongings – a jumble of spoons and forks, chairs, heavy clothing and jewellery – and selling them for whatever they could get.

They walked the wide, straight, gravel streets of Melbourne, blinking dust from their eyes. They had entered a frontier town. Tanneries lined the banks of the Yarra, and new arrivals baulked at the smell of dead flesh. Dogs roamed the streets in packs, horses were hitched to veranda posts and gold brokers displayed rough chunks of gold in their windows. This was the town that had lost 38 of its 40 policemen to the goldfields. It had lost gaolers and public servants. Public works were abandoned and buildings left unfinished. Over and again the place would fill to bursting with new arrivals and then empty dramatically as they left for the goldfields.

On almost every corner stood a pub where successful miners drank and boasted, while out the back every bed and scrap of floor was taken up by newcomers headed for the goldfields. Edward and Henry struggled to find a place to sleep. When they finally found two beds at Hockin's Hotel, on the corner of Elizabeth and La Trobe Streets, they were plagued by bed bugs. They left at dawn to begin the 60-mile walk to the goldfields.

They set off along the well-worn tracks of the Keilor Plains. Around a thousand men a day were making this journey. The *Mount Alexander Mail* compared the traffic on the road to Collins Street, and described a roadside littered with broken cart wheels, dead animals and pieces of clothing. Surrounding the trail was open bushland – dry and crooked eucalypts with pale trunks, and a blazing sun above. Sulphur-crested cockatoos screamed like banshees overhead. Passing kangaroos – which bore no resemblance to sheep or deer or horse – appeared like animals from myth. The two men stopped at Digger's Rest and Gisborne. There was constant talk of gold, and of the bushrangers who would tie you to a tree, steal your money and leave you for dead. At night Edward and Henry slept with a rifle between them, beneath the limitless gold of the stars.

The pitted and pockmarked landscape of the Forest Creek diggings. Photograph by Richard Daintree, c. 1850s.

They arrived at the Forest Creek diggings and found a ravaged brown landscape; earth stripped of trees and pitted with holes. Men and tents and huts seemed to cover every surface. Tens of thousands of men, boring into the land like termites. The noise was constant: spades hitting dirt, axes striking wood, wheelbarrows rolling over rocks. Every morning began and every night ended with men firing rounds from their rifles – a warning to robbers.

Edward and Henry bought their mining licences at once, then took a few days to look around. It seemed there were no places left to dig – none close enough to the creek, which they would need in order to wash the dirt. When they finally selected a claim – a piece of land about 12 x 24 feet – it was over a mile from the creek. They had to trek from claim to creek and back, over and over, in dusty, fly-plagued heat. When it rained, they worked in boot-sucking mud. They found a little gold; enough to fill a pill bottle. Then they got sick. Fever, cramps and painful diarrhoea. Edward recovered after a few days, but Henry just got sicker. Blood and faeces poured out of him. It was dysentery, common at the diggings where water was muddy and tainted by human excrement. Nothing could help Henry. Edward watched his only friend die.

It's here that Edward's story diverges from the tens of thousands of other gold seekers'. Edward did not keep dreaming of gold, and he did not go home to the hop-fields of Kent. He helped to bury his friend, and then he took another look around. He saw the incredible amount of trade being done in the camp; the huge sums paid for tools and clothes and food. So he sold his claim and tools, and bought a cauldron, a frying pan and a hard-to-come-by case of lemons.

On the frying pan he whitewashed the words 'Cole's Cordials'. He boiled water in the cauldron until it was safe to drink. And then he added the lemons – hoping their flavour would give him an edge over his competitors. It did. His pale yellow brew proved better than gold, and he began to pocket real profits.

On 4 January 1853, Edward turned 21. Alone and far from home he was proving to be a natural entrepreneur. He was also keen to do good. With vision and heart he had struck gold in his own way. But gold is always a risky business.

2 LIFE OF A DRIFTER

By January 1862, Edward was drifting along the Murray River in a flat-bottomed rowboat, dazed with heat, miles from anywhere and almost broke. His cordial money was long gone. He'd used it to buy land at one of the first Castlemaine land sales in 1854, helped along by the savings of his dead friend Henry Smith. Heavy rain and new wells were by then supplying plenty of clean water to the goldfields. Cordial was history, and gold digging little more than gambling. Land must have seemed like a very solid prospect.

The flat-bottomed rowboat that took Edward and George 1500 miles down the Murray River in the summer of 1861–62. Photograph by Edward Cole and George Burnell, c. 1862.

Edward had bought five town lots, sold three of them, and used the rest of his capital to begin building houses on the remaining two lots. He had no carpentry or bricklaying experience but, with an excess of optimism, he taught himself to cut timber and lay bricks. By the end of 1854 he had finished building a solid brick house.

Then the economy slumped. Instead of selling at a loss, Edward decided to ride it out. He borrowed money from the bank, using his one finished house as security, and began building a shop and dwelling on the second lot. But the bank foreclosed on his loan and sold the little home he'd built with his own hands.

It must have hurt. After two years of living in tents, he had now lost a house; it wasn't just an investment, but security and a roof over his head.

But Edward was determined to finish his project. He continued to build the shop and dwelling on the second lot, and took on extra jobs to pay for the materials. He took any job he could – selling fruit and vegetables, lighting lamps, and even returning to the diggings to sell more cordial. Somehow he even found time to attend meetings and debates at the Castlemaine Mechanics Institute. It was there that he met and befriended a man named George Burnell.

George was married with two children, and worked in the local corn and hay store. He also happened to own something most people in Castlemaine, most people anywhere, had never seen before: a camera. One day while in the Burnells' neatly kept shack, George showed the camera to Edward, and explained how he might start a business with it. He showed him how to prepare the chemicals for the glass plate, take a photograph and develop a print. Edward watched the image appear – perhaps an ordinary tree or wooden shack – with amazement. It must have seemed like freezing the very air, slicing out a square and preserving the scene it contained forever. The possibilities were staggering. Suddenly an entire family, a newly discovered country, even history itself, could be captured, quickly and simply, by this incredible tool. George asked Edward if he'd like to join him in a business enterprise. The camera stood on its tripod in the basic tin shack like an artefact from the future. Edward wouldn't just be selling photographs, but progress itself. How could he resist?

They purchased a horse and cart and lettered their names, Cole and Burnell, across the canopy. Edward rented out his almost completed shop and dwelling to a butcher (from whom he'd never receive a cent) and they left the town of Castlemaine behind them.

Of course, there was no great demand for photography.

They set off for the Forest Creek diggings, hoping to take portraits of the diggers who were dreaming of glory. But this was 1861, and while men still worked the earth, the swagger and posturing of the early years was gone. What would a digger do with a self portrait, perfect in every detail from his wayward beard to the dirt caking his moleskin trousers? So Edward and George, abstainers both, began approaching the pubs. They found that men with a few drinks under their belts were more willing to have their photos taken. They also took pictures of the pubs and sold them to the publicans to hang above their bars.

Occasionally they received commissions from wealthy squatting families. But work was still hard to come by. George believed he'd be better off establishing his own studio in Adelaide, and he wanted to travel there and see it for himself before uprooting his family. So the men headed for Echuca, and the mighty Murray paddle steamers that could take them to Adelaide.

Aborigines of Point McLeay mission at Lake Alexandrina, South Australia in 1862. Photograph by Edward Cole and George Burnell, c. 1862.

A rare photograph of an Aboriginal bark canoe in the making.
Photograph by Edward Cole and George Burnell, c. 1862.

They reached Echuca in December 1861, and found
that the wide brown river was too low for paddle steamers.
If they were to catch a steamer, the locals told them, they
would need to go to Wentworth, hundreds of miles away,
where the river was higher. Instead, the two men traded
their horse and cart for a leaky and cumbersome flat-
bottomed rowboat. They plugged the holes, built a couple
of bunks, rigged a canvas cover and set off on their very own
Murray River cruise. They were explorers: ready for discovery,
surprise, adventure.

At first they were keen to see it all. They would go ashore in the cooler mornings or early evenings. George would go hunting for Mallee fowl, kangaroo and bandicoot for their dinners. Edward went foraging for native seeds, plucking hard berries and flowers and coaxing seed-pods from their branches. Edward noted his finds in his diary. While most Europeans saw the Australian bush as an obstacle, something to be cleared in order to graze sheep or cultivate smooth green lawns and neat pines, Edward dreamed of creating a native garden. (In fact, he would later give the seeds to Baron Ferdinand von Mueller, who sowed them in the Melbourne Botanic Gardens.) They met Aborigines living along the river, and photographed them making bark canoes on the riverbank. Edward, curious as to their true number, planned to record all the Aborigines he encountered in his diary. Meanwhile, the boat drifted easily, and they hardly needed to row.

Which was lucky. Nothing had prepared them for the Mallee heat. A relentless sun pinned them beneath the canopy of their boat and poached them in sweat. Flies swarmed on their damp skin from dawn till dusk, when the mosquitoes took over. Edward abandoned his Aboriginal census. He stopped writing in his diary. On shore, they encountered bleached sand hills, mallee scrub, and the occasional sheep station, where they probably came across the bleak, pitiful forms of dead sheep struck by an outbreak of scab disease.

After four months and nearly 1500 miles of drifting in their old rowboat, Edward and George reached Lake Alexandrina in South Australia, from where they could travel by coach to Adelaide. The camera belonged to George; Edward would have to start planning his own future. With more seeds than money in his pockets, he would need to come up with something good.

3 THE PIEMAN'S EDUCATION

After months of flies, sweat and bandicoot meat, Edward and George found themselves in the small, orderly town of Adelaide. George had family there – his father was a church deacon and owned a tanning factory. While George assessed the town's commercial possibilities, Edward looked to his own commercial interests and made his way to the Adelaide Post Office for that crucial rent cheque from the butcher in Castlemaine. Only there was no cheque.

With no income, no job and little money, Edward was relying on the Burnell family's hospitality. But instead of looking for work, Edward went to the public library at the South Australia Institute to spend a day reading.

During their long days on the river, sharing the feverish air beneath the boat's canopy, Edward and George no doubt spoke about religion. It was a natural and familiar topic for them both – George's father and Edward's stepfather had both been Christians heavily involved in church life. At Lake Alexandrina, Edward met George's brother-in-law, the Reverend Taplin, who ran a Christian mission for Aborigines. They had gone to church there alongside Aborigines dressed in oddly matched and badly fitted European clothing, and later watched the same group perform a tribal death ceremony. Edward questioned the Reverend about the teachings of Christianity, and learnt from him a little about Aboriginal customs and beliefs.

Edward had begun to believe that all religions shared the same fundamental characteristics, and at the library in Adelaide he began to investigate this idea. He read every book he could on non-Christian religions, thrilling at any sign of common ground between them all. This too was exploration, with its sudden rush of discovery. After a single day he'd run out of books. If he wanted to pursue his ideas he would need to go to Melbourne, with its bigger and better public library.

Meanwhile, George was ready to open his photographic studio and was preparing to return to Castlemaine to collect his patient wife and small children. Edward wished him a good life and made his way to Melbourne.

This was not the city that Edward had seen in 1852. In the decade since, the population had increased fivefold, by then numbering 126,000 people. The city boasted a university, public library and art school. Many of the ramshackle wooden buildings had been replaced by double-storey stone or brick buildings with wide verandas. The swampland to the city's east had been transformed into the Botanic Gardens – then an orderly, geometric park. But for all its sophistication, the city stank. Three-foot-wide gutters ran with tannins, dyes and entrails from nearby factories, as well as raw sewage. Horse dung piled up on Bourke and Elizabeth Streets, and boys were paid a pittance to pick it up. Herds of cattle, sheep, pigs and goats were regularly driven down Bourke Street, while stray goats and pigs wandered the city, ruining gardens and occasionally attacking people.

The city had grown too fast; it had the trappings of a modern metropolis without the infrastructure to support it. The economy had shifted from wool to gold in the blink of an eye, and brought with it a massive influx of immigrants. By 1862 the economy was readjusting; wages were low and jobs scarce. Many people had left the goldfields for Melbourne, only to find themselves scrabbling for the lowliest, worst paid jobs.

Edward scrabbled too. He wove baskets in exchange for food scraps, and once even ate a meal of boiled grass and leaves before finally getting some labouring work on a building site. Sick of hand-to-mouth living, he saved up his money and bought a street barrow.

It must have felt like he was back at square one. His first job had been selling sandwiches on the streets of London at 17. Shy and fresh out of home, he'd struggled on those filthy, teeming streets. He'd been up against hundreds of hawkers, all tougher and more experienced than he was, calling out everything from sheep's trotters to hot green peas in their complex street slang. Melbourne's streets were now bustling with hawkers of every kind too, selling flowers, fruit and vegetables, fish, skinned rabbits, live cockatoos, Turkish delight, oysters and patent medicines. It would have been just as tough as London except for one thing: Edward was no longer a timid farm boy.

After a short stint selling pies from his barrow, Edward set up in a tiny shop front on Russell Street, near the corner of Little Bourke Street. The space was so small he could just squeeze his barrow in to form a countertop, and at night he slept on a bed beneath it. But its location was perfect. He was at the hub of Melbourne's nightlife and was surrounded by gambling houses, billiard rooms, pubs, the opium dens of Chinatown and the brothels in the red light district around Little Lonsdale Street. It was the drunks, the revellers, the prostitutes, petty criminals and larrikins who were out at night, in the half-lit, garbage-strewn streets. And when they got hungry, Edward was there with his 'delicious mixed meat pies'. His nights were soon filled with rowdy banter, rotten teeth and women in bright satin dresses, while his days were spent in the airy, white-columned quiet of the public library.

A Chinese opium den as depicted in an early edition
of *Cole's Funny Picture Book*.

The Melbourne Public Library stood, with its wide
frontage and Corinthian columns, like a misplaced piece
of the Acropolis, on a gently sloping lawn at the corner of
Swanston and La Trobe Streets. And, unlike most other
libraries at the time, admission was free.

After snatching a little sleep in the bed beneath his pie
counter, Edward would go to the gas-lit comfort of the
library's reading room. This was a favourite haunt of many
tired and street-soiled men who, after washing their hands
with library soap, took to sleeping in the quiet alcoves,
book in hand. Edward, however, kept his eyes open and read.

Edward read like a dog hunts rabbits – following his
nose, intuitive and obsessive. He sniffed out history,
science, philosophy and horticulture; he chased poets and
geographers through the pages of books. But the real prize
was religion. Here, finally, were books on every religion

The Public Library, Melbourne, showing Joseph Reed's design for the whole façade with the two corner pavilions. Lithograph by Henry George De Gruchy and Stephen Thomas Leigh, c. 1858.

he could imagine: Buddhism, Judaism, Confucianism, Parseeism, Mahometanism and more. Here was the proof of their shared humanity: their similar origin myths, instructions to do good and morality tales. They seemed more alike than different, and Edward must have been elated – he believed he had found the sort of knowledge that might encourage tolerance and understanding between men of all nations. He resolved to write his own book on the subject.

Edward also joined a free discussion society. Suddenly he was meeting people who passionately debated the issues of the day: evolution, vegetarianism, temperance,

cremation as well as religion. He was introduced to Spiritualism which, as it claimed to offer scientific evidence of the
afterlife through séances, appeared like the perfect bridge
between science and religion. (Later on he joined the Eclectic
Association, to which future prime minister Alfred Deakin
and writer Marcus Clarke, both Spiritualists, also belonged.)
Edward was watching debates, researching, writing and
giving papers to test out his own ideas. At night he would
return to the pie shop: to bawdy jokes, bursts of drunken
singing and the occasional street fight.

The intellectual life was intoxicating. Edward soon ditched
his pies and began selling books – first from his barrow and
then from a stall at the notorious Paddy's Market. Here
he had to trade above the terrified squawking of ducks for
sale, the calls of fishmongers and cheering from the shooting
gallery.

He also finished his book, *The Real Place in History of
Jesus and Paul*, in which he outlined the beliefs of the
major world religions, challenged the idea of their divine
origins, and argued for their recognition and morality.
No publisher would touch it. Not only had Edward put
other religions on a par with Christianity, he argued for
Christianity without God.

It was a disappointing end to two years' work. On the
bright side though, he was now the proprietor of a book stall
and the author of a serious book. This was not pies, cordials,
bandicoot meat or gold digging, the desperate means of

survival. This was ideas, knowledge and the elevation of the mind – the means with which to change the world. It was a brand new life for E.W. Cole.

THE REAL PLACE IN HISTORY OF JESUS AND PAUL

E.W. Cole, Melbourne, 1867

A missionary, in speaking of the doctrines of Christianity to a Hindoo priest, instanced, as one proof of their truth, the miracle of Jesus walking on the sea. The Hindoo replied that he also took miracles as evidence of the truth of his faith; but that his divine teacher wrought a greater miracle still – that he drank up the sea one night and vomited it again the next morning; and that consequently this being the larger miracle, his doctrine was the most true.

In the peninsula of Spain, 16,000,000 people tell us that the miracles of Jesus are an evidence of the truth of Christianity. Cross the straits of Gibraltar, a few miles in width, and 10,000,000 people give us the miracles of Mahomet as an indubitable evidence of the truth of the doctrines of Mahometanism. No! although the men of nearly all the religious creeds throughout the world attempt to prove the truth of their doctrines by relating the miracles of their founder and his disciples, yet the fact remains that a miracle is no evidence whatever of the truth of any doctrine; nay, more, a doctrine that requires miracles to make men accept it, is unworthy of the acceptance of man. Doctrines worthy of the acceptance of man when once uttered, render themselves glaringly apparent by virtue of their own inherent force, beauty, and truthfulness, so that all reflecting men throughout the earth, of whatever creed, cannot but admit their truthfulness and intrinsic worth.

4 TALL TALES

But this was not exactly the quiet, contemplative life of a bookman and scholar. Paddy's Market was a jumble of food stalls, entertainers, pickpockets, live animals, preachers and soapbox orators. Officially called the Eastern Market, and located on the corner of Bourke and Stephen Streets (now Exhibition Street), it was the major supplier of fresh food to the burgeoning city. On Saturday nights, when it stayed open late, a swarm of tradesmen, miners, revellers, families and vagabonds would gather beneath its corrugated zinc roofs in search of fun. Discarded oyster shells were crunched to grit underfoot, and gaslight and Chinese lanterns spilled their light into the darkness.

And there – amid the blaring brass band, Chinese gongs, yapping dogs and howls from the Punch and Judy shows – was Edward, trying to promote the quiet pleasures of reading. He put up signs announcing 'Cole's Cheap Books' and 'A free pen with every purchase.' He made sure no one was hurried along or asked to buy, and he slowly built a business. But with the circus in full swing around him, he also began to learn about show business.

He could see that if he wanted to get noticed he had to make some noise. But he wasn't about to start spruiking his books by yelling over the top of the fishmongers and hot-nut sellers. Edward would shout in his own way.

In 1873 he placed an ad in the *Herald*'s classifieds section, which in those days occupied the front page of the newspaper. Among column after column of product listings and basic descriptions was his sensational heading 'Discovery of A Race of Human Beings with Tails'. Edward's ad described the tail-bearing natives apparently encountered by an explorer in the dense interior of New Guinea. Known as the Elocwe, these rare beings were two-legged, immensely hairy and indisputably human. The writing was scientific in tone, and supported by quotes from Darwin's *Descent of Man*. It concluded by promising that more would appear in Monday's paper.

The first Eastern Market as depicted by Charles Troedel in 1864. By 1869, Edward occupied stall no. 1 next to the Haymarket Theatre.

FURTHER PARTICULARS RESPECTING
THE RACE OF HUMAN BEINGS WITH TAILS

E.W. Cole, *Herald*, Melbourne, 30 August 1873

[Mr Jones] refers to the thousand and one tail pains and the thousand and one tail pleasures that the Elocweans respectively suffer and enjoy, and he asks himself the question, is it best or not to have a tail? After enumerating the many mental and corporeal sufferings that the Elocweans undergo from ugly tail, deformed tail, diseased tail, jammed tail, frostbitten tail, burnt tail, scalded tail, rheumatic tail, crushed, mangled, and sore tail from all causes, and tail pains of all kinds, besides the enormous cost of keeping it clothed, doctored, decorated, &C., he seems more than half inclined to congratulate himself that he has escaped much suffering from being, in spite of his rudimentary tail, practically tailless; but upon passing in review the numberless ecstatic delights, extra sensations and pleasures, mental and corporeal, that the Elocweans enjoy in consequence of having that extra member, and accepting the principle that the pleasurable sensations of our members always exceeds the pains, and therefore, the more members we have the more we enjoy, he finally and positively concludes that taken all in all, the good with the bad, that the Elcoweans, in possessing another important organ, are the most happy people in the world, and that it is best for man to have a tail.

Monday's paper was a sell-out. By planting this curious story among the bland listings for soap and insurance agents, Edward had hijacked the public's attention. He had not mentioned a single product or the name of his business. But for those paying close attention he'd named himself – albeit backwards – in the name of the tribe.

Every day of that week, from Monday to Friday, a new notice appeared. Each one illuminated some aspect of Elocwean society, from tail fashion and customs, to tail hygiene, and even tailomancers – those gifted sages who could read the future from tail hairs.

On Saturday, the final instalment appeared. It invited all tailless inhabitants of Melbourne to go to Cole's Cheap Book Store at the Eastern Market, where they would find for sale a great variety of TALES.

Edward was suddenly the talk of the town. He was a minor celebrity and a genuine market attraction, and more people than ever came to visit his stall. His plan had worked brilliantly.

These were heady times for Edward, and no less for the city itself. With a population of over 200,000 people, and gold money filling the coffers, Melbourne's appetite for entertainment, consumer goods and expensive new buildings was enormous. In 1870 the simple brick building on the corner of Swanston and Collins Streets that had served as the Town Hall was replaced by a classical, Second Empire building with a clock tower and two grand organs.

In 1872 Melbourne got its own Royal Mint on William Street, and the Palazzo-style Customs House on Flinders Street was finished in 1876.

In this spirit of delirious progress, and after years of complaints from stallholders about the lack of proper shelter, the city council decided to tear down the ramshackle Paddy's Market and build a grander, more permanent market in its place.

It was bad timing for Edward. After years of living hand to mouth he was finally making a place for himself. He had no desire to move. But upheavals also create new openings, and Edward had a talent for spotting them.

He found a vacant shop just ten doors down from the market. The building was long, low and gloomy and he threw all his money and energy into an ambitious renovation. Edward was a fan of the Royal Arcade further down Bourke Street, with its glass roof, palm trees and easy atmosphere, where people could promenade or window shop out of the elements and without pressure to buy. This was the effect he was aiming for, and he even called his new shop Cole's Book Arcade. He installed a light well, gas jets, mirrors and cane chairs, and he widened the entrance. He painted the shop-front white, with a giant coloured rainbow curving over the entrance.

Then he registered the rainbow as his trademark.

5 SHE MUST BE SOBER

In 1875 Edward was a handsome 43-year-old who wore his beard long and was always neatly dressed. His Book Arcade was thriving, and he'd taken on several employees to help him in the shop. When he wasn't working, he loved to sit in on discussion groups and debates. But there was no sign of a wife, girlfriend, romantic interest, thwarted love or childhood sweetheart. Nothing at all. The first sign finally showed up in July 1875 when, among the notices for Homeopathic Chocolate and Doctor Scott's Bilious and Liver Pills, the following notice appeared:

A GOOD WIFE WANTED
Twenty Pounds Reward

I, EDWARD WILLIAM COLE,
Of the
BOOK ARCADE
BOURKE-STREET,

wish to obtain a person for a wife with the following characteristics:–

SHE MUST BE A SPINSTER of thirty-five or six years of age, good tempered, intelligent, honest, truthful, sober, chaste, cleanly, neat, but not extravagantly or absurdly dressy; industrious, frugal, moderately educated, and a lover of home. Any respectable, well-intentioned person who from the range of their observation can conscientiously recommend to me an unegaged woman answering the above description will, in the event of a marriage taking place between us in consequence of such information, receive my sincere thanks, and the above reward directly [should] such marriage take place. This may be thought by many an absurd, because unusual, way of looking for a wife; and I am quite sensible that I may be laughed at, but the thoughtful will not laugh, the most that they will do in that direction will be to smile good-humoredly, for they know that whilst the best thing a man can have is a good wife, and the worst thing a bad wife, yet, in most cases, a very irrational principle of selection is followed, for that nineteen out of every twenty of the unions that take place originate from the merest accidents of life, from a chance meeting at a ball, at a relation's, at a friend's, at a neighbour's &c. I take what I believe to be the more reasonable course, of looking wide around to find, and when found, of ascertaining, by inquiry, the exact character a woman bears in her neighbourhood, and amongst those who know her, before I enter into indissoluble intimacy with her: and I have no more hesitation in advertising for, and critically examining into the character of one who is to be my partner for life, than I should have were I merely advertising for a business partner: and if, by advertising, I get a good, a sensible, and a suitable wife instead of an unsuitable one, which I very likely should get in the usual way, my temporary exposure is well indemnified and my twenty pounds is well spent.

Please address any communication to E. W. COLE,
Book Arcade,
Bourke-street

N. B.–The strictest of confidence is of course guaranteed to all correspondents.

E.W. Cole, *Herald*, Melbourne, 3 July 1875

In 1875 one did not advertise for a wife in the classified section of the newspaper. And one certainly did not offer a financial reward to the successful candidate. The public reaction was split between amusement and outrage, and many thought it simply another of Edward's publicity stunts.

He read through all the responses, some berating him for taking lightly the holy state of matrimony. But Edward was absolutely serious. One reply in particular caught his attention:

> Sir,
> I have very carefully read your letter in the Herald and I think it a very sensible one.
>
> For my part I think it a very serious thing to get married, and if there were more thought as I do, I think there would be fewer unhappy unions.
>
> I have been a little over twelve months in Victoria. I am a Tasmanian, and if ever you have visited that island you could not but remark the difference between the people there and here, so sociable and friendly. People here tell me I should not say I come from Tasmania because of unfortunate aspects of its history, but I will stick up for my island home as long as I have breath, for my family are highly respectable, and there has never been a stain on one of our names.
>
> I thought I would tell you I was a Tasmanian in the first place, for you might be one of the narrow-minded ones, though I hardly think so by your sensible remarks. I have made the acquaintance of a few gentlemen in Victoria, and what I have met do not come up to my ideas of a good husband. I do not care so much about a pretty face (though I like to see one as well as most people). I would sooner have good sense and good temper any day. I am not pretty myself, for I am a little dark thing with dark eyes and hair, and nearly thirty years old.

*I want someone to love and take care of me, someone I
can look up to and respect, one who is good-tempered, sober,
good-principled, industrious, honest, and kind, and I am
sure it will not be my fault if I do not make him a good wife.*

*I have received a very good education, and have been
brought up to do everything from making a pudding to
playing the piano. I am rather hard to please, for I tend
to look before I leap. You could not blame me for that.
So if you think you would like to make my acquaintance
you can do by addressing a letter to*

Tasman,
Post Office,
Melbourne
And I will see you if you wish it.

Edward replied to Tasman's letter and no other, and asked
her to come and see him at the Book Arcade. Like a comedy
of errors, Edward sweated on the prospect of Tasman's visit,
then happened to be out of the Arcade when she came by.
It might have ended there, if Tasman had been a demure
Victorian lass. But Tasman had backbone; she penned
another note then and there:

Mr Cole,
I have just called and feel too nervous to wait till you come in.

*I would like to see you and have a quiet talk with you as you
wished. I do not like to call again, but I will meet you this
evening at seven o'clock at the top of Collins Street in Spring
Street. (I will be dressed in a dark dress with black hat and rose
at side so you will be able to distinguish me.) When you speak
call me Tasman, then I will know it is yourself.*

I remain,
Tasman

The woman with the rose and black hat was Eliza Jordan: plump, plain and forthright. A month later they were married.

Edward and Eliza would go on to have six children, a succession of cats and dogs, mutual friends, several overseas trips and, by all accounts, share a very happy life together.

Eliza Cole

Edward Cole at 40

6 A WHITE ELEPHANT

When Melbourne's new Eastern Market opened in 1879 it was an impressive sight: a fully enclosed, split-level Italianate building skirted by cast-iron verandas and lit by glass skylights. It was also virtually empty. When Paddy's was demolished, market gardeners, poultry vendors and fishmongers were forced to relocate to the Queen Victoria Market, and had come to like it there. Few could be enticed back. Without the pyramids of winter apples, the smell of ripe cheeses and the rowdy choir of hawkers and hagglers, and with only a sad handful of traders occupying the vast, echoing building, the Eastern Market had become a ghost market.

Edward watched the market with interest. He'd always loved the western end of Bourke Street, where the Opera House, Theatre Royal and the Royal Arcade drew the biggest crowds. A thriving market could attract more of those people to the top end of Bourke Street, which would take them right past the doorway of Cole's Book Arcade. But the market remained an expensive, empty shell.

Then Edward had the wild idea of leasing the entire market himself. He knew the old market, and thought he knew how to put the lifeblood back into it. He approached the market's agents and, after handing over £2000 for one year's lease and a £500 sweetener, Edward found himself running the Eastern Market.

Edward knew it was vital to get the stallholders back, and quickly. The market needed a barrage of noises, smells and sights – the primal reek of fish, the grotesque faces of Punch and Judy, the whip-crack of rifle shot – in order to come alive. So he offered the stalls rent-free for six months.

He welcomed the market's former fruit and vegetable sellers as well as entertainers of every stripe. He hired a brass band to play every afternoon, and crammed extra lighting and display cabinets into the stalls.

Before long, the market was a chaotic junction of food, sideshows and some truly bizarre performances. There was a

Saturday Night at the Eastern Market by David Syme and Co., 1888.
1. *A Good Shot.* 2. *Active benevolence.* 3. *Nice bird, sir – will you buy?*
4. *A satisfactory test.* 5. *"War Cry, a penny."*

live dental show performed by the Great American Painless Dentist. There were Madame Xena's Shilling Shocks from Scientifically Controlled Electricity – Guaranteed to Double Male Vitality. Phrenologists discovered a subject's true personality in the shape of their skull, and Madame Zinga Lee read their future in the tarot. A lady wrestler battled any man who tried to land a kiss on her, while jugglers kept all their balls in the air. And for the young toughs, Charlie the Tattoo Man marked the passage to manhood with his pierced red hearts and sultry mermaids.

Edward sent out a flyer telling the people of Melbourne it was their duty, as citizens of this excellent city, to visit their 'Grand Market and Meeting Place Every Saturday Night'. But there was nothing dutiful about the crowds that swamped the market week after week. As soon as the rent-free period ended, Edward began to profit nicely. He had backed his wild idea, and was now collecting £10,000 a year in rent from the stallholders.

Melbourne City Council had spent £100,000 building the new market, and they were keen to recoup their investment. Within a few years they refused to renew Edward's lease, declaring they would call for tenders instead. No tender was accepted. Instead, the council took over the lucrative lease and directly pocketed the rent.

Edward had single-handedly reinvented the Eastern Market. Another businessman might have taken the council to court or at least expressed bitterness over the loss, but Edward accepted the situation without complaint. He might have loved a challenge, but he abhorred conflict. And he could afford to walk away: the Book Arcade and Eastern Market had proved that he could make something out of nothing. He didn't need Madam Zinga Lee to tell him the future was bright.

The [New] Eastern Market. Engraving by Alfred May and Alfred Martin Ebsworth, 1878.

In the late 1880s, Edward Cole ventured to make 'a few small predictions' for what life might be like in the year 2000. Far from being small, his predictions were for fundamental and far-reaching changes for the entire world, and suggested a utopian outlook and incredible optimism. Some have even come true.

PROPHECIES FOR THE YEAR 2000

E. W. Cole, Melbourne, c. 1880s.

Flying machines will be in general use, passing and repassing every point on earth

A network of railways, telegraphs, telephones, and later inventions will cover the entire earth, bringing nearer together, associating, and fraternizing all nations

All savage and barbarous races will be subjugated by more advanced nations, civilised, and then allowed the rights of equals

One federated and comprehensive language, with English as a base, and enriched with the best and most expressive words adopted from all other languages, will be spoken generally throughout the world

One sensible religion, including a belief in immortality, will be believed in generally throughout the world

The reasonable rights of women will be established throughout the world

The land of the world will become the property of all the people of the world

The earth will yield four times what it does now

The yearly average of real honest labour will be no more than six hours per day

Everybody will easily obtain proper food, clothing, and the necessaries of life

Crime will be diminished one-half

Drunkenness will be almost banished from the earth, and habitual drunkards treated as lunatic

The average length of life will be nearly doubled

Men will feel that eating, drinking, sleeping, dressing, playing, and money making are not the sole purpose of life; but that they are destined for something higher and nobler

The world will be federated in politics, in religion, and in language. And men will wonder why they were fools so long

READREADREADREADREADREADREADREAD
READREADREADREADREADREADREADREAD
READREADREADREADREADREADREADREAD

COLE'S
NEW
BOOK
ARCADE
WILL
OPEN ON
CUP DAY.
It is the
FINEST SIGHT
In
MELBOURNE,
And the
GRANDEST
BOOK
SHOP
IN
THE WORLD.
Intellectual
non-racing
People
are
invited
there
instead
of going
to the
RACES.

READREADREADREADREADREADREAD
READREADREADREADREADREADREAD
READREADREADREADREADREADREAD

7 BLUEPRINT FOR UTOPIA

By the age of 50, Edward Cole had gone from hawking old books from a barrow outside the Eastern Market to becoming the market's saviour, turning it into a rampant carnival and profitable business. He had married his newspaper bride, and she had already given him four children, on whom he doted. He had his Book Arcade and money in the bank. Edward could afford to take things easy. But it just wasn't in his nature.

Edward was interested in more than making money. He had written a book on religious tolerance, regularly attended debates and was the librarian for the Eclectic Association.

He was deeply interested in the fate of humankind, and closely followed the issues of his day such as Sunday trading, federation, temperance and universal suffrage. Two issues lay particularly close to his heart: the importance of books and the equality of mankind. Edward believed in a peaceful, happy, tolerant future society. For all his business acumen, he was a true idealist. With the Eastern Market back in the council's hands, he was free to imagine a project that could combine his idealism with his unique business talents.

Edward wanted a new location for Cole's Book Arcade. He longed for an abundance of space, somewhere big enough to accommodate all the ideas in his head. When he saw the old Spanish restaurant on Bourke Street – shabby and neglected – he thought he'd struck gold. It was a three-storey building, 90 feet wide and 120 feet deep. During the gold rush it had thrived, but its cavernous interior now dwarfed the few people who went there to dine. It could be gutted and a new structure built on its solid, bluestone foundations. And best of all, it was in the most popular stretch of Bourke Street – just a few doors up from the Royal Arcade.

With his characteristic blend of vision and action, Edward drew up his own building plans and supervised every detail of the building process. He kept the solid brick walls but replaced the roof with an arched iron and glass panelled roof of his own design that would drench the interior in

Cole's Book Arcade, photograph by George Rose, c. 1890s.

49

natural light. He removed the second and third floors to let the light through, and replaced them with circumambulatory balconies. He had his shelving custom built from cedar: above waist level were display shelves and below were deep filing drawers for extra storage of books – all labelled by subject so that customers could help themselves. He filled the ground floor with highly polished brass columns and mirrors, which multiplied in their own reflections and created the impression of a room without end. In addition to the book department, there were smaller departments for stationery, music and novelties.

The overall effect was of vast space, sun gilded surfaces and polished wood. It was a cross between a Victorian railway station and a grand cathedral, with its exaggerated height and length, curved ceiling and arched windows. Naturally, a large painted rainbow appeared across its white façade. Decorating the balconies were smaller rainbows bearing slogans such as 'The reign of knowledge and humanity is coming'.

Edward claimed to stock over a million books. His titles ranged from poetry to Marxism and sex education. For Edward, books were not just a business but a moral crusade. As one of his slogans proclaimed: 'The happiness of mankind, the real salvation of the world, must come about by every person in existence being taught to read and induced to think.' With this in mind Edward filled the Arcade's ground floor with over a hundred chairs. His policy was that anyone could read for as long as they liked without being disturbed.

The iron and glass ceiling that transformed a gloomy building into Edward's brightly lit 'Palace of the Intellect'.

Cash-strapped students, calloused tradesman and local hoodlums took to reading in these elegant cane-bottomed chairs. Some also took advantage of the relaxed supervision to steal books. The number of thefts was high compared to other stores, but Edward's response was philosophical: at least the thieves were reading. Edward also installed a lending library on the second level.

The Arcade was a dynamic business and its ever-expanding stock included perfume, musical instruments, confectionery and ornaments. Edward regularly added new departments, such as 'The Ornament Exhibition' on the top floor in 1885, and 'The Shilling Room' (where nothing cost more than a shilling) in 1893. He eventually bought or leased many of the adjoining buildings, until the Arcade spanned two city blocks – from Bourke Street all the way to Collins Street. He would stock anything that sold, got people talking or supported his favourite causes.

In 1895, in the heart of the depression years, Edward opened a Chinese tea salon in the Arcade. Unemployment was widespread, and he had no trouble finding Chinese waiters to serve the tea. It was a daring move. Not only had the depression slowed trading, it had also exposed strong racist, and particularly anti-Chinese, attitudes within the community. Edward wrote: 'The people everywhere, white or coloured, that you do not know, are as good as the people that you do know.' He hired a professional artist to paint murals of Mandarin palaces and tranquil ornamental lakes on the salon walls. He made the tea salon an everyday luxury. The tea arrived in expensive-looking Chinese teapots with matching cups, but the prices were always affordable. In spite of prejudice and poverty, the tea salon became a favourite destination of Melbournians.

In the late 1890s, Edward invited Indian hawkers to trade in Howey Place, the laneway that joined his Little Collins Street and Collins Street buildings. He also took on the unusual Simon Gabriel. Mr Gabriel suffered a rare skin

Edward had Howey Place paved and roofed at his own expense to link all the buildings of the Book Arcade. The roof remains today.

condition that had turned his skin from black to white. His primary role was to chat to people: if they could not tell by talking to him that he was really a black man, didn't it show that there was no difference between the races?

While Edward harboured a utopian vision, he never forgot the showman's lessons he had learned at the Eastern Market. Many of the Arcade's attractions were pure atmosphere. Wonderland, opened in 1893, was a department solely

The unusual Simon Gabriel as photographed in 1890 and 1897.

devoted to optical illusions and funny mirrors. In the deep shade of the fernery, where plants towered over six feet tall, cockatoos, parrots and their exotic cousins would punctuate nearby conversations with their shrill comments. And then there were the monkeys. Vociferous and quick limbed, they lived in a room on the upper level decorated with jungle scenes, but their rank animal odour permeated much of the Arcade. Originally a private hobby of Edward's, they were, like all aspects of his life, readily amalgamated into his eclectic store. Even his family, living in a flat on the top floor of the Arcade, were part of the show. Eliza commanded her own small corner of the Arcade, where she would sit and watch the passing crowd or entertain her friends for afternoon tea. The public knew this spot as Queen's Corner. On wet days, the family's laundry drying on the upper balconies was simply another strange sight for the customer who happened to look up.

Over four decades, Cole's Book Arcade became part of Melbourne's soul. For many, it was synonymous with the city itself. A trip to town meant a trip to Cole's, for afternoon tea, the latest book or to catch the monkeys in some rude act. It was like no other store in the world, for it was

Eliza seated at 'Queen's Corner', n.d.

not really like a store at all. It was an extension of Edward Cole himself, an expression of his unique ideas and passions. If Edward could picture the future as a harmonious Utopia, then the Arcade was its blueprint, mapping out the way it could be achieved.

If only the crowds that passed through Wonderland could have looked through the ceiling. Then, on certain nights, they might have seen a stout Victorian lady, modestly dressed in heavy velvets and high collar, sitting in the semi-darkness, speaking in a trance. They might have seen her, eyes closed and faintly sweating, surrounded by people holding hands and whispering questions or listening in rapt silence. Perhaps they might have heard mysterious knocking or felt a sudden chill breeze. They might, in short, have witnessed a séance. The woman, a self-proclaimed medium, was Eliza Cole, and the other participants were her friends and family, including Edward. They were Spiritualists, believers in an afterlife where the dead can communicate with the living. In Victorian society, Spiritualism was not only fashionable, it was quite respectable.

When not holding séances in the ballroom above Wonderland, Eliza loved to host novelty evenings there. She excelled in the role of the genial ringmaster, shepherding her guests into sing-alongs, charades, spelling bees and blind man's bluff.

8 COLE'S FUNNY PICTURE BOOK

Every good child should have one
for being good, and every bad child
should have one to make it good

Behind the publicity stunts and showman's antics, Edward was a shy and private man. He could have had his pick of Melbourne's social scene with its various balls and parties, but he was happiest at home with his children, delivering them armloads of fresh fruit for breakfast, or reading them Tom Sawyer's latest misdeeds. He would tend the rooftop garden above the Arcade, or sit and bounce a baby monkey on his knee, away from the gaze of the outside world.

Another of his quiet hobbies was filling scrapbooks with newspaper cuttings, funny pictures and poems. In 1879 he published what was essentially a giant scrapbook. He called it *Cole's Funny Picture Book*, and placed it for sale in the Arcade on Christmas Eve. It flew out the door. It would eventually sell around a million copies and become an icon for generations of Australians. Many people still have an image of Cole's Patent Whipping Machine for Flogging Naughty Boys burned into their memories. *Cole's Funny Picture Book* carried the trademark rainbow on its cover and was filled with a cut-and-paste collection of picture puzzles, stories, poems and rhymes taken from illustrated newspapers, periodicals and other publications of the Victorian era. There was also some original content, such as the whipping machine, a few serious essays such as one against smoking tobacco and Edward's favourite Book Arcade ads.

So how did a hotchpotch of borrowed rhymes, sermonising and blatant advertising become one of the best loved children's books in Australia? For a start, there simply weren't a lot of entertaining children's books on the market. Lewis Caroll's *Alice in Wonderland* had pioneered the fun, irreverent, illustrated children's book in 1865, but the genre didn't really take off until the 1880s, with the appearance of titles like Robert Louis Stevenson's *Treasure Island* (1883), Mark Twain's *The Adventures of Huckleberry Finn* (1884) and Rudyard Kipling's *The Jungle Book* (1894). In the meantime children's books tended to be instructive and moralistic. Willis P. Hazard's *A Home Book for Good Children* (1855) and Harriet Beecher Stowe's *Women in Sacred History*

(1873) are good examples: their titles alone suggesting a sternly moralistic approach to education.

The second reason for the popularity of *Cole's Funny Picture Book* was the price. Edward sold the first print run for only a shilling, a mere fraction above production costs. And, of course, Edward's offbeat and almost naïve humour struck a chord with the public.

The books were idiosyncratic and their contents changed between editions. In fact, Edward continued to treat the *Funny Picture Book* like his own personal scrapbook. He included essays on his favourite topics, such as 'What books do for mankind'. One page featured his son Vally with his clever dog; his daughter Ruby starred in another. When eight-year-old Ruby died suddenly of scarlet fever, Edward was heartbroken. He wrote a moving epitaph for Ruby's page in

OUR RUBY

Our dear little daughter once went to a children's ball dressed as a fairy. She was proud of being a fairy, and looked so nice that I put together the above nursery doggerel to please her, and in honour of the event, little thinking that she would so soon leave us for the other world. It might be considered better by some to remove this page, but as children like it I venture to let it stand with this explanation. - E.W.C

what could be considered a solemn addition to a 'funny' book for children. But, like the Arcade, the *Funny Picture Book* became an expression of much that lay closest to Edward's heart.

Edward also gained a fair reputation as a compiler. After adding a printing department to the Arcade, he produced books of songs and poems, gardening, wise sayings and doctors' advice. All displayed the distinctive rainbow cover. And while none ever matched the popularity of *Cole's Funny Picture Book*, they all contributed to making Cole a household name. Edward also bought up remaindered books and repackaged them with the rainbow cover, and produced cheap editions of classic works.

His approach to branding was, like most of his ideas, unconventional and ahead of its time. He started a minor collecting craze with his series of copper medals. The medals bore slogans such as 'Let the World Be Your Country' and 'To Do Good Be Your Religion'. The medals were given out free at the Arcade, and on several occasions Edward had to sell the medals as admission tokens to control large crowds. This was done to slow down rather than deter people, though it seems to have only added to their excitement.

Edward played a seminal role in Australian publishing, cranking out popular books that most people could actually afford. *Cole's Funny Picture Book* was groundbreaking, and has become an Australian classic – to this day writers and illustrators of children's books cite it as an influence. Not bad for a man who learned to read with his family Bible.

In the midst of the brass band playing, birds screeching and dense crowds, it was possible to spot the occasional celebrity at Cole's Book Arcade. In 1891, a man wearing small eyeglasses and an oversized, coal-black moustache visited the Arcade. He was Rudyard Kipling and, at 26 and even before the publication of *The Jungle Book*, already world famous. In 1895, many people would have recognised Mark Twain, with his wild eyebrows and famous scowl, drinking in the Chinese Tea Salon with Edward and Eliza. Edward, a passionate fan, could not wait to give Twain a copy of *Cole's Fun Doctor*, which featured so much of Twain's own writing. Twain begged Edward to keep the truth to himself; for while Australians thought of Twain as an original, he said, it would seem he owed many of his jokes to *Cole's Fun Doctor*.

One of Australia's leading poets, Frank Wilmot (aka Furnley Maurice), worked at the Book Arcade from the age of thirteen in 1894 until it was demolished in 1929. Friends from his literary and political circles, such as Guido Baracchi, founder of the Australian Communist Party, and the musicologist Henry Tate were always dropping by the Arcade. When Wilmot was asked how the management felt about his frequent visitors, he replied that they didn't mind, 'because, like the monkeys, it brought business'.

COLE'S
FUNNY PICTURE BOOK

Johnny Smith's father bought him
Cole's Funny Picture Book No. 1.

Emma Jones's step-mother wouldn't
let her have one.

TO **DELIGHT** THE **CHILDREN**
AND MAKE HOME HAPPIER

Our Pussies' Fan Dance.

Madam Grump and Her Babies

THE **BEST** CHILD'S **BOOK** IN THE **WORLD**
FIRST PUBLISHED
1879

Mother and Father disputing debating on what to Call the Baby.

PUZZLE.

It is   It is   town,

it has the m   renown,

t   the   was found;

the   around.

above the   ,

s gn wa   yet dis ed.

are   d with   its w s

at or   t by anyone t c .

w is most sure to

if U will c & C.

COLE'S PATENT WHIPPING MACHINE
FOR FLOGGING NAUGHTY BOYS IN SCHOOL

**COLE'S ELECTRO-MICRO SCOLDING MACHINE
FOR SCOLDING NAUGHTY GIRLS**

I, the undersigned, firmly believe that as man has already made machines to run over the land and float over the water faster than the swiftest animal, so shortly he will make machines to fly through the air as fast, and finally faster, than the swiftest birds do now. And I hereby offer a bonus of £1,000 to any person who shall (in consequence of said bonus) within the next two years, invent a flying machine, to go by Electrical, Chemical, Mechanical, or any other means, except gas, a distance of 100 miles, and shall come and stop in front of the Book Arcade, Bourke Street, Melbourne, Australia, as easily and as safely as a carriage stops there now.

E.W. Cole, *Herald*, Melbourne, 31 October 1882.

GO TO COLE'S BOOK ARCADE FOR THE FUNNIEST PICTURE BOOK IN THE WORLD

Meddlesome Jacko.

Here is the cat. *Find two Rats.*

9 THE WHOLE HUMAN RACE IS MIXING

Not all of Edward's books were popular. *The Real Place in History of Jesus and Paul* was rejected by every publisher he approached; in the end he could only give away copies of the manuscript. Despite the rejection, Edward continued to publish books and pamphlets, many of which were ignored or even derided by the public.

In the mid 1880s Edward published *The Federation of the World* – his first pamphlet in two decades. In it, he predicted that by the year 2000 the world would share one government, one language and one religion. He wrote:

'One sensible religion, including a belief in immortality, will be believed in generally throughout the world.' He placed it for sale alongside *Cole's Funny Picture Book* and *Cole's Fun Doctor*, but was disappointed when its sales lagged well behind his runaway comic successes.

In 1890 Edward ran an essay competition on the theme 'Federation of the Whole World'. He planned to compile the best responses into a book, and offered a £10 prize for the five best essays for and against the idea of a world federation. The prize-giving ceremony was held at the Arcade, where it turned out a writer for the *Bulletin*, James Edmond, won a prize for his essay in favour of federation and then, under a pseudonym, another for his essay against it. This comic turn of events did not help Edward to be taken seriously. The subsequent book of essays sold poorly, and Edward lost around £1000 on the project. He abandoned his plans for a follow-up volume.

But Edward was eventually compelled to pick up his pen again. In 1901 the Australian colonies became a federation. Edward was delighted. To him, federation signalled co-operation, unity and brotherhood. But the first major act before the new Australian parliament was the Immigration Restriction Act – otherwise known as the White Australia Policy. The act would not only restrict, but virtually abolish, all non-white immigration to Australia. The policy enjoyed popular support within the parliament and among the public.

Edward was appalled. He viewed the nation's first act as both selfish and short-sighted. This was not the tolerant and progressive future he had dreamed of for Australia. He wrote an impassioned argument against the policy in a pamphlet called *A White Australia Impossible and for Various Reasons Undesirable*. In it he pointed out that under the proposed law even Jesus would have been denied entry to Australia and concluded, 'no man can support this law and remain a Christian.' He quickly wrote a follow-up tract, *The Whole Human Race is Mixing and Must Mix*. These pamphlets sold reasonably well; and he also gave them away in large quantities, but the act still passed easily in parliament.

This caused great offence to the governments of India and Japan, and the Japanese Government lobbied hard to have the law amended.

In 1903 the Japanese Government invited Edward to attend the Fifth National Industrial Exhibition in Osaka. Presumably they wanted him to return to Australia singing the praises of a civilised and advanced Japanese nation.

So at the age of 71 Edward set off with his wife, eldest daughter Linda and youngest daughter Ivy for six months in Japan, China and the Pacific. He was ushered into meetings with dignitaries and heads of government, interviewed by the press, taken to exhibitions and museums and palaces. Edward was in his element. The Japanese media hailed him as a writer, philosopher and prophet; in Australia he was simply the eccentric Cole of the Book Arcade.

Wherever he went, Edward handed out a special Japanese edition of one of his medals. In turn, the Coles were presented with gifts and tokens of friendship; Ivy was given a pedigree poodle named Wai, which stood for White Australia Impossible.

On his return, Edward immediately conveyed his experiences in a pamphlet. *What 40 Eminent Japanese Say of the White Australia Act* drew a scathing response from the *Herald* – the newspaper in which Edward advertised most heavily. A leading article headed 'No Piebald Australia' declared 'Australia's policy is to preserve our island continent for the white man, and the view of Japanese statesman, whether four, forty or four hundred, will not affect us one whit.' Edward's pamphlets were not selling well either, and he resorted once more to giving them away.

Instead of giving up he wrote more: *The Better Side of the Chinese Character* and *The Oneness of Man*. He kept trying to find new ways to demonstrate the good qualities inherent in all races. He repackaged his essays and bookended them with jokes and poems and pictures, sugarcoating the serious content. He used all the resources at his disposal and showed no fear of alienating the customers on whom he depended. Edward had his sights on a more tolerant and harmonious future: on Utopia itself. Offending a few customers was a small price to pay.

Of course some of his material would strike a modern reader as both racist and sexist. Edward did not believe

The Coles on their return from Japan. Eliza and Edward are on either side of the captain, Ivy is holding the Japanese dog and Linda is behind the captain. c.1903

women should be given the vote. He thought that black and Asian immigrants should populate Northern Australia because 'white man cannot work in the tropics ... white women become wrecks in the tropics ... white children cannot be reared in the tropics.' While he wrote in support of many races around the world, he showed no consideration for the treatment of Australian Aborigines. But he genuinely believed that people the world over were equal, and that they had an equal right to health, security and happiness. His fight against the White Australia Policy was passionate and sustained. Did he really believe we would someday see an end to wars, poverty and hatred? Perhaps he believed it was best to live as though we would.

30 STRONG REASONS WHY "A WHITE AUSTRALIA" IS IMPOSSIBLE

E.W. Cole, *The Smallest Newspaper in the World*, Melbourne, n.d.

1. Because every 7th person in the Commonwealth is already more or less coloured, and gradually many will blend.
2. Because the sun is the cause of skin colour.
3. Because all Australians will in time become coloured.
4. Because the white man cannot work in the tropics.

5. Because white women become wrecks in the tropics.

6. Because white children cannot be reared in the tropics.

7. Because the coloured man must develop the tropics.

8. Because Jesus Christ was a coloured man.

9. Because Jesus taught the universal brotherhood of man.

10. Because humanity exists in every human heart.

11. Because the feeling of human kinship is universal.

12. Because all mankind are capable of inter-blending.

13. Because all mankind are inter-blending everywhere.

14. Because the British people are for universal freedom.

15. Because the British Empire has 7 coloured to 1 white.

16. Because the Act is an insult to all coloured nations.

17. Because Australia will tire of being a laughing stock.

18. Because Australia's home humanity is against the Act,
    and all Christian teaching is, must, and will be against it.

19. Because the Act is against the interests of commerce.

20. Because the Act prevents the development of Australia.

21. Because our white birth-rate is diminishing.

22. Because enough white emigrants will not come so far.

23. Because we are surrounded by coloured people.

24. Because Australia has 100 times the area of Scotland and a
    few million of white people have no right to monopolize it.

25. Because Japan, China, India, and Java are awakening.

26. Because China has 400 millions and is overflowing.

27. Because India has 300 millions and is overflowing.

28. Because Java's 30 millions are very near to Australia.

29. Because the whole world belongs to those who need it.

30. Because God has made mankind of one flesh and blood.

FEDERATE THE WORLD

FEDERATION OF THE WORLD
ONE GOVERNMENT
ONE RELIGION
ONE LANGUAGE
ONE COINAGE
BEFORE THE YEAR 2000

HUMANITY IS PROGRESS
THE REIGN OF IGNORANCE AND FORCE IS GOING
THE REIGN OF KNOWLEDGE AND HUMANITY IS COMING

THE GOVERNMENT OF RIGHT
THE RELIGION OF GOODNESS
ENGLISH LANGUAGE IMPROVED BY THE BEST WORDS OF ALL OTHER LANGUAGES

FULL ACQUAINTANCE ONLY REQUIRED
IF ALL MEN THROUGHOUT THE WORLD WERE WELL ACQUAINTED WITH EACH OTHER THERE WOULD BE LITTLE OR NO WAR FOR THEN ONLY THE MOST WICKED WOULD HAVE TO BE KEPT IN ORDER BY THE WORLD'S POLICE
E.W.Cole

FRIEND
IT IS YOUR DUTY AS ONE OF THE HUMAN FAMILY TO HELP TO FEDERATE THE WHOLE WORLD OTHERWISE ASSIST TO MAKE ALL MANKIND HAPPY

FEDERATION OF THE WHOLE WORLD
AT THE RATE MANKIND ARE NOW PROGRESSING IN LITERATURE, SCIENCE, EDUCATION, COMMERCE, POLITICS, MORALS, HUMANITY, FRIENDLY INTERCOURSE AND PRACTICAL COMMON SENSE THE EARLY FEDERATION OF THE WORLD IS INEVITABLE

UNITED STATES OF THE WORLD
TIS COMING TIS COMING
ONE GOVERNMENT
ONE RELIGION
ONE LANGUAGE
BEFORE THE YEAR 2000

76

10 THE END OF THE RAINBOW

In 1912 it was not uncommon for the residents of Essendon to see an old man in a silk top hat and long white beard riding in an immaculate horse-drawn brougham with his pet marmoset scampering around the carriage. The old man was Edward Cole, travelling from Earlsbrae Hall, his Essendon mansion, to his Bourke Street Book Arcade. Edward was now a widower; Eliza had died the previous year following surgery on her leg. It had been almost 36 years since she had answered a wanted ad, which she thought a 'very sensible one', in the *Herald* newspaper. Edward had lost his most loyal friend, confidant and life companion. He had also lost his reason for living above the Arcade – it was Eliza who had loved city living and insisted they remain there. When Edward suffered a stroke, his doctor advised him to move from the city.

After a lifetime of modest living, 80-year-old Edward found himself a palatial double-storey residence named Earlsbrae Hall (now Lowther Hall Anglican Grammar School). With sixteen Corinthian columns, 53 plate glass windows and 27 rooms, there was plenty of room for all his children and their spouses. For extra company he brought along his favourite monkeys from the Arcade and gave them the run of the place. They were soon joined by a bulldog, a kangaroo and an aviary full of songbirds. The grounds were covered in green lawns and palms trees, and Edward added a 75-foot floral rainbow. This was country living, as original and unexpected as every other life that Edward had lived. There were Sunday night singalongs, dinners and more séances. A stuffed polar bear in a nickel cage served as a hat stand. Charity groups held fundraising fetes and bazaars on the lawns. Life at Earlsbrae was vibrant and, with his family, his monkeys and a garden of his own, Edward should have been the image of contented old age.

But Edward was troubled by his legacy. The stroke was a clear and constant reminder of his mortality. What would he leave behind?

He began work on an impossibly ambitious publishing project, *The Cream of Human Thought Library*. The idea was to bring together the finest writing in the world – 1000 books on 1000 subjects. But the real issue was the Arcade. What would become of it?

For years the Arcade had been run according to Edward's idiosyncrasies. There was no formula, no neat business plan, just his natural business instincts and generous heart. Who on earth could succeed him?

Edward sweated on the matter for months. He chose his eldest daughter Linda, his son-in-law Rupert Rudd (married to Ivy), his bank manager Charles White, and his long-serving department head, Henry Williams.

Edward Cole died in his bed on 16 December 1918 at the age of 86, watched over by his sons and daughters. In his room he had constructed a series of mirrors so that he could the see the rainbow flower beds while lying down. Apart from his family, the rainbow was probably one of the last things he ever saw.

Above: Edward with one of his marmoset monkeys, c. 1910s
Opposite: Bourke St looking east from the GPO, c. 1880s.
Previous page: Edward with his family at Earlsbrae Hall, his home at Essendon, c. 1910s.
Next page: the Little Men welcomed customers at the Arcade's Bourke Street entrance. Photograph by Spencer Shier, c. 1890s.

READ

LENDING LIBRARIES

COLLINS ST. 6000 Volumes.   BOURKE ST. 2000 Volumes.

EPILOGUE

Within ten years of Edward's death, Cole's Book Arcade had run itself into the ground. The properties were sold and the Arcade demolished. It had been Edward's great fear that the Arcade would not long survive him; that he would have no legacy. Perhaps it was inevitable. A generation growing up with Luna Park and talking pictures would have demanded different entertainments.

All that remains of Cole's Book Arcade today is the glass and iron roof above Howey Place, where Indian hawkers once traded. But hundreds of thousands of people visited the

Arcade over the years. They read and borrowed and bought books that influenced or moved them. Some laughed at their faces twisted in the funny mirrors or at the brazen self promotion of *Cole's Comic Advertiser*, when they may have had little else to laugh at. This is E.W. Cole's quiet legacy: intimate and impossible to measure. But it is a legacy all the same.

Edward would probably not mind that his own story has nearly been forgotten. He was used to people not taking him seriously. But it's remarkable how often he goes unmentioned in the histories of Australian advertising, bookselling and publishing, and in relation to the White Australia Policy. His is one of the great stories of Marvellous Melbourne. Now that you have taken the time to read it, the tale of Edward Cole will live a little longer.

Above: Edward outside Earlsbrae Hall. Photograph by Spencer
Shier, c. 1910s. Previous spread, left: Edward at work in his
office, n.d. Previous spread, top right: Arcade management after
it closed, L–R: Jack Smith, Henry Williams, Syd Endacott,
c. 1929.Previous spread, bottom right: the only known
photograph of the Arcade band, n.d.

BIBLIOGRAPHY

Annear, Robyn, *A City Lost and Found: Whelan the Wrecker's Melbourne*, Black Inc., Melbourne, 2005.

Bellanta, Melissa, 'Clearing Ground for the New Arcadia: Utopia, Labour and Environment in 1890s Australia', *The Journal of Australian Studies: New Talents/ Jumping the Queue*, no. 72, 2002.

Benjamin, Walter, *The Arcades Project*, Harvard University Press, Massachusetts, 2002.

Brandon, Ruth, *The Spiritualists: The passion for the occult in the nineteenth and twentieth centuries*, Weidenfeld & Nicholson, London, 1983.

Brown-May, Andrew, *Melbourne Street Life*, Australian Scholarly Publishing, Kew, 1998.

Brown-May, Andrew and Swain, Shurlee (eds), *The Encyclopedia of Melbourne*, Cambridge University Press, Melbourne, 2005.

Campbell, Colin, *The Romantic Ethic and the Spirit of Modern Consumerism*, Basil Blackwell Ltd, Oxford, 1987.

Carrol, Brian, *The Australian Advertising Album*, Macmillan, South Melbourne, 1975.

Clark, Manning, *A History of Australia, vol. V*, Melbourne University Press, Carlton, 1981.

Cole, Edward, *Cole's Funny Picture Book*, no.1, Cole Publications, Melbourne, n.d.

Cole, Edward, *The Cream of His Thoughts: Selections from the writings of Edward William Cole*, A.B. Cole, Melbourne, 1916.

Cole, Edward, *Federation of the World*, E.W. Cole, Melbourne, c. 1880s.

Cole, Edward, 'Papers', Manuscripts Collection, State Library of Victoria.

Cole, Edward, *The Real Place in History of Jesus and Paul*, E.W. Cole, Melbourne, 1867.

Cole, Edward, *A White Australia Impossible and For Various Reasons Undesirable*, E.W. Cole, Melbourne, 1901.

Curthoys, Ann, 'Truth and Fiction in History', *Dissent*, Summer 2003–04.

Davison, Graeme, *The Rise and Fall of Marvellous Melbourne*, Melbourne University Press, Melbourne, 1981.

Docker, John, *The Nervous Nineties: Australian cultural life in the 1890s*, Oxford University Press, Melbourne, 1991.

Dixon, Robert, *Writing the Colonial Adventure: Race, gender and nation in Anglo–Australian popular fiction 1875–1918*, Cambridge University Press, Melbourne, 1995.

Flannery, Tim (ed.), *The Birth of Melbourne*, Text Publishing, Melbourne, 2002.

Forster, H.W., *The Central Gold-fields*, Cypress Books, Melbourne, 1969.

Gabay, A., *Messages From Beyond: Spiritualism and spiritualists in Melbourne's golden age 1870–1890*, Melbourne University Press, Carlton, 2001.

Hall, Rodney, 'Being Shaped By The Stories We Choose From Our History', *The Alfred Deakin Lectures: Ideas for the future of a civil society*, ABC Books, Sydney, 2001.

Hocking, Geoff, *Castlemaine: From camp to city 1835–1900*, Five Mile Press, Rowville, 1994.

Hocking, Geoff (ed.), *Early Castlemaine: A glance at the stirring fifties*, New Chum Press, Melbourne, 1998.

Kruithof, Mary, *Fever Beach: The story of the migrant clipper Ticonderoga*, QI Publishing, Mt Waverley, 2002.

Lewis, Miles, *Melbourne: The city's history and development*, City of Melbourne, Melbourne, 1995.

Macartney, Frederick, *Furnley Maurice*, Angus and Roberston, Sydney, 1955.

McCalman, Iain, 'Flirting with Fiction', McIntyre, S. (ed.), *The Historian's Conscience: Australian historians on the ethics of history*, Melbourne University Press, Carlton, 2004.

McCann, Andrew, *Marcus Clarke's Bohemia: Literature and modernity in colonial Melbourne*, Melbourne University Publishing, Melbourne, 2004.

Morrison, Ian, *The Vandemonians: From penal settlement to Marvellous Melbourne*, Ginninderra Press, Charnwood, 2005.

Pyke, A.D., *The Gold, The Blue: A history of Lowther Hall*, The Council of Lowther Hall Grammar School, Essendon, 1983.

Richards, Thomas, *The Commodity Culture of Victorian England: Advertising and spectacle 1851–1914*, Stanford University Press, Stanford, 1990.

Sparrow, Jeff, *Communism: A love story*, Melbourne University Press, Carlton, 2007.

Sparrow, Jeff, 'From the Archive: When Anarchy Came to the Great Southern Land – The Bizarre Story of Utopias, Dystopias, and Political Penny Dreadfuls in Nineteenth Century Melbourne', *Arena*, Dec 2002.

Sparrow, Jeff & Sparrow, Jill, *Radical Melbourne: A secret history*, Vulgar Press, Carlton North, 2001.

Turnley, Cole, *Cole of the Book Arcade*, Cole Publications, Melbourne, 1974.

Williams, Henry, *E.W. Cole: An Appreciation*, Book Arcade Printing Department, Melbourne, c. 1916.

Illustrations
All illustrations from *Cole's Funny Picture Book*, no. 1, Cole Publications, Melbourne, n.d., except p. vi and p. 76 from Cole, Edward, *Federation of the World*, E.W. Cole, Melbourne, c. 1880s, p. 30 from Cole, Edward, *Cole's Intellect Sharpener*, E.W. Cole, Melbourne, c. 1890s, and p. i, 12, 15, 16, 24, 28–29, 37, 38, 41, 42–43, 49, 51, 53, 54, 55, 73, 79, 80, 81, 82, 83, 84 and 85 from Pictures Collection, State Library of Victoria.

www.arcadepublications.com